Your World

Buses

Decomposing Numbers 11–19

Logan Avery

Grandma and I
ride the bus.

It will be a fun day!

We get on the bus.

20
people

There are 20
people on our bus.

The first stop is uptown.

17
people

3 people exit.

The next stop is downtown.

15
people

2 people exit.

The next stop is near the park.

12
people

3 people exit.

The next stop is
near our house.

10
people

Grandma and
I exit.

Goodbye, everyone!

Goodbye, bus!

Problem Solving

People stand and sit inside buses. Each bus has 10 people standing. Write how many people are sitting.

Bus	Total People	People Standing	People Sitting
A	11	10	
B	14	10	
C	19	10	

Answer Key

A: 1 person

B: 4 people

C: 9 people

Consultants

Nicole Belasco, M.Ed.
Kindergarten Teacher, Colonial School District

Colleen Pollitt, M.A.Ed.
Math Support Teacher, Howard County Public Schools

Publishing Credits

Rachelle Cracchiolo, M.S.Ed., *Publisher*
Conni Medina, M.A.Ed., *Managing Editor*
Dona Herweck Rice, *Series Developer*
Emily R. Smith, M.A.Ed., *Series Developer*
Diana Kenney, M.A.Ed., NBCT, *Content Director*
June Kikuchi, *Content Director*
Véronique Bos, *Creative Director*
Robin Erickson, *Art Director*
Stacy Monsman, M.A., and Karen Malaska, M.Ed., *Editors*
Michelle Jovin, M.A., *Associate Editor*
Fabiola Sepulveda, *Graphic Designer*

Image Credits: All images from iStock and/or Shutterstock.

Library of Congress Cataloging-in-Publication Data

Names: Avery, Logan, author.
Title: Your world : buses / Logan Avery.
Description: Huntington Beach, CA : Teacher Created Materials, [2019] | Audience: K to Grade 3.
Identifiers: LCCN 2017059903 (print) | LCCN 2018009256 (ebook) | ISBN 9781480759640 (e-book) | ISBN 9781425856267 (pbk.)
Subjects: LCSH: Arithmetic--Juvenile literature. | Subtraction--Juvenile literature. | Counting--Juvenile literature. | CYAC: Arithmetic. | Subtraction. | Counting. | LCGFT: Picture books. | Instructional and educational works.
Classification: LCC QA115 (ebook) | LCC QA115 .A92 2019 (print) | DDC 513.2/1--dc23
LC record available at https://lccn.loc.gov/2017059903

Teacher Created Materials
5301 Oceanus Drive
Huntington Beach, CA 92649-1030
www.tcmpub.com

ISBN 978-1-4258-5626-7